MASKS

EDWARD BRATHWAITE

Masks

LONDON
Oxford University Press
NEW YORK   TORONTO
1968

Oxford University Press, Ely House, London W.1.
GLASGOW NEW YORK TORONTO MELBOURNE WELLINGTON
CAPE TOWN SALISBURY IBADAN NAIROBI LUSAKA ADDIS ABABA
BOMBAY CALCUTTA MADRAS KARACHI LAHORE DACCA
KUALA LUMPUR HONG KONG TOKYO

© *Oxford University Press* 1968

PRINTED IN GREAT BRITAIN

FOR
MY MOTHER AND FATHER
AND MICHAEL MY SON

ACKNOWLEDGEMENTS

Acknowledgements are due to the Editor of the Poetry Book Society *Supplement*, 1967, and the BBC Third Programme, where material from this poem was first used.

A Glossary of some of the Akan words used in the text will be found on page 77.

Only the fool points at his origins with his left hand.
Akan Proverb

I
Libation

I
Prelude

Out
of this
bright
sun, this
white plaque
of heaven,
this leaven-
ing heat
of the seven
kingdoms:
Songhai, Mali,
Chad, Ghana,
Tim-
buctu, Volta,
and the bitter
waste
that was
Ben-
in, comes
this shout
comes
this song.

Gong-gongs
throw pebbles in the rout-
ed pools of silence: news
of ripples reach the awakened Zu-
lus: Chaka tastes
the salt blood of the bitter
Congo and all Africa
is one, is whole, nim-
tree shaded in Ghana,
in Chad, Mali,
the shores of the cooling kingdoms.

Beat heaven
of the drum, beat
the dark leaven
of the dungeon
ground where buds are wrapped
twist-
ed round dancing roots. White
salt crackles at root lips, bursts like a fist
and beats out this
prayer:

Nana Firimpong
once you were here
hoed the earth
and left it for me
green rich ready
with yam shoots, the
tuberous smooth of cassava;

take the blood of the fowl
drink
take the *eto*, mashed plantain,
that my women have cooked
eat
and be happy
drink
may you rest
for the year has come round
again.

Asase Yaa,
You, Mother of Earth,
on whose soil
I have placed my tools
on whose soil
I will hoe
I will work
the year has come round
again;

thirsty mouth of the dust
is ready for water
for seed;

drink
and be happy
eat
may you rest
for the year has come round
again.

And may the year
this year of all years
be fruitful
beyond the fruit of your labour:
shoots faithful to tip
juice to stem
leaves to green;

and may the knife
or the cut-
lass not cut

me; roots blunt,
shoots break,
green wither,

winds shatter,
damp rot,
hot harm-

attan come
drifting in harm
to the crops;

the tunnelling
termites not
raise their red

monuments, graves,
above the blades
of our labour.

II
The Making of the Drum

I

The Skin

First the goat
must be killed
and the skin
stretched.

Bless you, four-footed animal, who eats rope,
skilled
upon rocks, horned with our sin;
stretch your skin, stretch

it tight on our hope;
we have killed
you to make a thin
voice that will reach

further than hope
further than heaven, that will
reach deep down to our gods where the thin
light cannot leak, where our stretched

hearts cannot leap. Cut the rope
of its throat, skilled
destroyer of goats; its sin,
spilled on the washed gravel, reaches

and spreads to devour us all. So the goat
must be killed
and its skin
stretched.

2

The Barrel of the Drum

For this we choose wood
of the *tweneduru* tree:
hard *duru* wood
with the hollow blood
that makes a womb.

Here in this silence
we hear the wounds
of the forest;
we hear the sounds
of the rivers;

vowels of reed-
lips, pebbles
of consonants,
underground dark
of the continent.

You dumb *adom* wood
will be bent,
will be solemnly bent, belly
rounded with fire, wound-
ed with tools

that will shape you.
You will bleed,
cedar dark,
when we cut you;
speak, when we touch you.

3

The Two Curved Sticks of the Drummer

There is a quick
stick grows in the for-

est, blossoms twice year-
ly without leaves;
bare white branches
crack like light-
ning in the harm-
attan.

But no harm
comes to those who live near-
by. This tree, the
elders say, will never
die.

From this stripped tree
snap quick sticks for
the festival. Its wood,
heat-hard as stone,
is toneless as a bone.

4

Gourds and Rattles

Cal-
abash trees'
leaves

do not clash;
bear a green
gourd, burn
copper in the
light, crack
open seeds
that rattle.

Blind underground the rat's
dark saw-teeth bleed
the wet root, snap
its slow long drag of time,

its grit, its flavour; turn
the ripe leaves sour. Clash
rattle, sing gourd; never leave
time's dancers weary like this tree
that makes and mocks our music.

5

The Gong-Gong

God is dumb
until the drum
speaks.

The drum
is dumb
until the gong-gong leads

it. Man made,
the gong-gong's
iron eyes

of music
walk us through the humble
dead to meet

the dumb
blind drum
where Odomankoma speaks:

III

Atumpan

Kon kon kon kon
kun kun kun kun
Funtumi Akore
Tweneboa Akore
Tweneboa Kodia
Kodia Tweneduru

Odomankoma 'Kyerema se
Odomankoma 'Kyerema se
oko babi a
oko babi a
wa ma ne-ho mene so oo
wa ma ne-ho mene so oo

akoko bon anopa
akoko tua bon
nhima hima hima
nhima hima hima . . .

Funtumi Akore
Tweneboa Akore
Spirit of the Cedar
Spirit of the Cedar Tree
Tweneboa Kodia

Odomankoma 'Kyerema says
Odomankoma 'Kyerema says
The Great Drummer of Odomankoma says
The Great Drummer of Odomankoma says

that he has come from sleep
that he has come from sleep
and is arising
and is arising

like *akoko* the cock
like *akoko* the cock who clucks
who crows in the morning
who crows in the morning

we are addressing you
ye re kyere wo

we are addressing you
ye re kyere wo

listen
let us succeed

listen
may we succeed . . .

II
Path-finders

I
Mmenson

Summon now the kings of the forest,
horn of the elephant,
mournful call of the elephant;

summon the emirs, kings of the desert,
horses caparisoned, beaten gold bent,
archers and criers, porcupine arrows, bows bent;

recount now the gains and the losses:
Agades, Sokoto, El Hassan dead in his tent,
the silks and the brasses, the slow weary tent

of our journeys down slopes, dry river courses;
land of the lion, land of the leopard, elephant
country; tall grasses, thick prickly herbs. Blow elephant

trumpet; summon the horses,
dead horses, our losses: the bent
slow bow of the Congo, the watering Niger...

II

Axum

With the help of the Caliph
of Heaven, who in heaven
and earth conquers all;

I, El Hassan, son of Amida,
King of Axum,
of Halen, Hemer, Rayden and

Salhen;
made war on the Noba;
fought at Takazi, by the ford

of Kemalke;
burnt town, destroyed
villages, pillaging

houses and temples
whether of stone or of straw
did not matter; splattered

blood in the corn;
burnt their altars of horn,
bronze and copper; threw

their dark wooden gods in the river
and the next day moved on
till we reached the Red River . . .

III
Ougadougou

And I, Ougadougou,
sprawled on the Niger,
watched them come:

red whispering walls moving,
smoke squeezing our eyes,
cinders sneezing. The heat

was before us; mirages danced
in its silver; our brittle walls
crumbled, flat walking roofs

tumbled; red tongues
licked grass from the streets,
children screamed, women ran,

crackled sparks' eyes crashing to ashes;
goats butted and turned, blinded; horses
stamped. Where are the dancers,

the flutes' reed voices
cut from the river, the songs'
achievement of cymbals?

They come riding, porcupine driving
our errors before them; too soft,
too blandished, too ready for peace and for terror.

IV
Chad

This sacred lake
is the soul
of the world;

winds whirl
born in the soul
of this dark water's world.

This lake
moulds
the wars of the world;

no peace in this world
till the soul
knows this dark water's

world.
Reeds whisper
here in the morning;

buffaloes blaze;
and around these shores,
man whirls

in his dark rest-
less haste; search-
ing for hope; seek-

ing his fate
far from the shores
of this lake.

V
Timbuctu

Whose gold you carry, camel,
in this cold cold world?
Whose pearls of great price?
Whose cinnamon, whose spice?

Your world of walls, o city
of my birth, rises so certain
so secure; the plains
of dust surrounding us

so kept away, so distant.
Whose gold you carry, camel,
on your hill-top back?
To what far land you now

transport our wealth?
And what wealth here, what
riches, when the gold returns
to dust, the walls

we raised return again
to dust; and what sharp winds,
teeth'd with the desert's sand,
rise in the sun's dry

brilliance where our mosques
mock ignorance, mock pride,
burn in the crackled blaze of time,
return again to whispers, dust.

VI
Volta

My lord, all this time since we left
Walata, you have led these people. Are you not
tired?

I am very tired, Munia. My head
aches, my feet
are weary; sometimes
the light seems to sing before my face.
My blood cries out for rest.

But still you won't rest
you won't give up. Can't we
stop here? Have we
not travelled enough?

The young men murmur, El
Hassan; the women
long for a market
where they can chatter and laugh.

I know, I know.
Don't you think that I too know
these things? Want these things?
Long for these soft things?

Ever since our city was destroyed
by dust, by fire; ever since our empire
fell through weakened thoughts, through
quarrelling, I have longed for

markets again, for parks
where my people may walk,
for homes where they may sleep,
for lively arenas

where they may drum and dance.
Like all of you I have loved
these things, like you
I have wanted these things.

But I have not found them yet.
I have not found them yet.
Here the land is dry, the bush
brown. No sweet water flows.

Can you expect us to establish houses here?
To build a nation here? Where
will the old men feed their flocks?
Where will you make your markets?

So must we march
all the time?
Walk in this thirsty sun
all the time?

There is a land, south
of here, where it is richer.
I have heard tales told
of the mouths of great rivers

that smile; of forests
where farms may be broken;
deep lakes in these forests;
and plains where our cattle

may graze; and further on,
a place where the water
boils white at its whispering
edges.

White?
The water?

Hot
at its edges?

Is it not
Naderina, of which
the sages speak?

Perhaps
perhaps
the weak mind only seeks
towards these things

in dreams, in cracking sun-
light's visions; but I heard
the sound of silver run-
ning with the clink of water

as if a river were flowing
soft and always south from here.
For miles the land was brown and dry
for miles clear sky

and rock; three days we travelled, dream-
ing; heavy tongues dumb, soles and our ankles
numb, foreheads shocked with heat.
The land was empty and the

rainless arch of nothing stretching stretched
straight on. Three days we travelled, in-
steps knotted, chords of our thighs' flesh frayed
and muscles afraid of the next hot step, the next hot

slipping stone; three days we travelled
to that low sky morning when we saw the mist,
grey sticking breath,
nosing the blind earth;

heard the whisper, knew
the ground now soft and softer,
growing grassed and greener,
till we reached the White River . . .

III
Limits

I
The Forest

1

Like walls the forest stops us.
Over the ford at Yeji it was waiting:
tangled squat mahogany out-
riders and then the dense, the
dark green tops, bright
shining standing trunks:
wawa, dahoma, esa and
odum; the doom
of the thick stretching green.
Leaves gathered darkness; no
pathway showed the way.
The trunks grew tall and
taller, dark and darker; earth
now damp, fern cool, moss
soft. We hacked our way
through root and tendril, climber
shoot and yellow clinger. This
was the pistil journey in-
to moistened gloom. Dews
dripped, lights twink-
led, crickets chirped and still
the dark was silence, still
the dark was home. We
scorched, we raked, we
settled; cleared path,
cut clearing, burnt the dry rot
out of withered wood to make this farm.
And at night, so that no harm
would come from dark still heavy on us,
made this fire: fire-
flies from sticks, from cinders; and we
sang:

in praise of those who journey
those who find the way

those who clear the path
those who go on before us

to prepare the way.

We sang of warmth and fires,
bodies touching, eyes of embers, watching.

Where are the open spaces now
clear sky, the stars, horizons' distances?

We sang of warmth and fires,
bodies safe and touching.

2

But the lips remember
temples, gods and pharaohs,

gold, silver ware; imagination
rose on wide unfolded wings.

But here in the dark,
we rest:

time to forget
the kings;

time to forget
the gods.

That fat man
with the fire-

light's grease
that dances

on his belly—
belly button

bunged—is he
the king

or glutton?
He lives

on human
blood

and dies
in human

blood;
our empire's

past of stone
and skulls

demands it.
And Ra,

the sun
god's gold,

demanded blood
to make it

sacred.
Time to forget

these kings.
Time to forget

these gods.
The jewelled sun

has splintered
on these leaves.

The moon-
light rusts.

Only the frogs wear jewels
here; the cricket's chirp is

emerald; the praying mantis'
topaz pleases; and termites'

tunnel eyes illuminate the dark.
No sphinx eyes close and dream

us of our destiny; the desert
drifting certainties outside us.

Here leaf eyes shift, twigs
creak, buds flutter, the stick

becomes a snake; uncertainties adrift
within us.

3

So praise the new eyes,
leaves' butterflies, flies'
sympathy; the dark trees
understand.

Raise the mantis face, my
brother; mother tree, your
rough bark mocks me
but we understand.

For night of leaves and leaves
of stars and stars' winked darkness
is a new world of discovered here;
new world of time and time's uncertainty.

II
Adowa

1

So that with new warm arms the forest holds us.
From this womb'd heaven comes the new curled god
with goblin old man's grinning, flat face smiling,
crouched like a frog with monkey hands and
insect fingers. This we will carve and carry
with our cooking pots, wood mud and wattle;
symbol sickness fetish for our sickness.
For man eats god, eats life, eats world, eats wickedness.
This we now know, this we digest and hold;
this gives us bone and sinews, saliva grease and sweat;
this we can shit. And that no doubt will ever hit
us, the worm's mischance defeat us, dark roots
of time move in our way to trip us; look, we dance:

2

No whirl of the flute
here;
bamboo shoots
flar-
ing the dryness;
no high yodel steel
in the brightness;

into the shift of the darkness,
mud-flowered heel
stamping the softness, dare
we now the fanged roots'
whisper and lisp of our fear's
darkness, tender and mute?

But slowly our daring uncurls the mute fear; hands whisper and twist into movement; buttocks shift stones of inertia; rhythms arise in the darkness; we dance

and we dance on the firm earth; certainties, farms, tendrils unlocking; wrong's chirping lightning

no longer harms us; birds echo what the earth learns; and the earth with its mud, fat and stones, burns in the tunnelling drum of our hot timeless morning, exploding dimensions of song.

III
Techiman

1

The path through gloom, dark
drip-

ping through star-
wet leaves' crevices,

will not soon
turn to light, set

like a square window; will not let
in the free sail of night's moon

that voyages the Arab's roomy
heaven.

Here green's net sticks
wet, clings soft sweet comfort cunning

like Ananse's tune-
less, once Onyame's, trap of doom.

2

But the way lost
is a way to be found
again;

the moist
stones, warm
pebbles of rain,

move into tossed
leaves of darkness; round
my mud hut I hear again

the cry of the lost
swallows, horizons' halloos, found-
ationless voices, voyages . . .

Techiman drizzles in sun-
light; Peki peeps
out of the valley; fun-
loving Nsuta sleeps

in the misty, water-
well'd dawn. Burn
Koforidua, holy tree
blasted by lightning; turn

in your sleep, sleepers
at Krachi; the almond leaves
scratching your rocks, rock
you awake for new journeys; stop-

ping at Golokwati, Kpandu and Pong
for rest, salt and water;
then onward to Teshie,
Labadi, Kaneshie . . .

Time's walking river is long.

IV
The White River

1

From the Akuapim ridge un-
rolled a new land.
Hands on the hoe
knew new grasses:

nkyekyere and lemon;
and the bold knocking demon
of darkness was tamed on the Akropong rocks.
Light rounded to flesh

at Aburi; and the hills
of the Ga lands: Akuse
and Shai: were like islands
burning to green in the water of pastures;

plains drowned in the shallow
drifting of cloud. Crowds
flocked to the Volta, darker
at Ada; and over we ferried

to the hard, sandy gold of Keta.
Here at last was the rager,
the growler, wet breather,
life giver, white curly smoker,

time's river, rushing for-
ever: round pebbles, carved musical
shells; wet ropes in the tide,
tugging moon's motion;

wet sails in the salt; winds drying
the sand into powder; drying
fish, glittered silver;
guinea cock's eyes of their scales in the dark

wood of boats: forest trees fallen and scooped
with tongue's fire; canoes reaping danger;
sharp shark's teeth's death-whiteness ready;
at the slow sloping ledge of our village; time's water's

edge; the white river.

2

This was at last the last;
this was the limit of motion;
voyages ended;
time stopped where its movement began;

horizons returned inaccessible.
Here at last was the limit;
the minutes of pebbles drop-
ping into the hourless pool.

Hands reached into water;
gods nudged us like fish;
black bottomless whales that we worshipped.
O new world of want, who will build the new ways,

the new ships?

IV

The Return

I
The New Ships

1

Takoradi was hot.
Green struggled through red
as we landed.

Laterite lanes drifted off
into dust
into silence.

Mammies crowded with cloths,
flowered and laughed;
white teeth
smooth voices like pebbles
moved by the sea of their language.

Akwaaba they smiled
meaning welcome

akwaaba they called
aye kooo

well have you walked
have you journeyed

welcome.

You who have come
back a stranger
after three hundred years

welcome.

Here is a stool for
you; sit; do
you remember?

Here is water
dip
wash your hands
are you ready
to eat?

Here is plantain
here palm oil:
red, staining the fingers;
good for the heat,
for the sweat.

Do
you remember?

2

I tossed my net
but the net caught
no fish

I dipped a wish
but the well
was dry

Beware
beware
beware

I travelled to a distant town
I could not find my mother
I could not find my father
I could not hear the drum

Whose ancestor am I?

I walked in the bush
but my cut-
lass cut

no path;
returned
from the farm

but could not hear
my children
laugh.

Beware
beware
beware

For now the long hot flint-
locks sing with heat;
fever of quick sales
rot the branches

of bone; blood brands the bird's
full sails and trinkets
sear my flesh. Whose
brother, now, am I?

Could these soft huts
have held me?
Wattle daubed on wall,
straw-hatted roofs,

seen my round or-
dering, when kicked to life
I cried
to the harsh light around me?

If you should see someone
coming this way
send help, send help, send help
for I am up to my eyes in fear.

3

And beware
cried Akyere
do not trust strangers.
In their watery eyes
I see dangers.
Hooks jerk
in their smiles,
lurking capture;
sticks
from their stares
are a dry beach
of sand's pain,
bleaching bones
of despair,
your life's
fear.

Do not trust
strangers.
Smell the danger:
cassava cooked
skin that the
wind brings;
their sin
stretches like
smoke, dis-
appears in the white
wind, but re-
mains, re-
mains to stain
our truth with its
stench; and when
night comes,
when night
comes, chok-
ing my eyes'
throat, the fire

is drenched
in fright's
phantoms:
sasabonsam
of darkness
where even the deep-
est drum trembles.

So beware
cried Akyere
beware
the clear
eyes, the near
ships, the
cast lines,
sweet cargoes
of promises.
Beware the steer'd
smiles, their
teeth's rock,
the white
fathoms.

4

But our women,
pepper-
eyed, glad to see

strangers, will-
ing to sell
gold, fleshes'

thighs for tin
trinkets, thin
cloth stamped

with flowers;
our elders,
kola-nut-

chewing,
showing
gums stained,

tarnished
with drugs'
greed, love of

profit, for-
got the grey
gods of anger

who warned
against smiling
hands groping

for markets, not
wor-
ship; for-

got the long wars
brought us here
in the gossip

of who pleases
Portuguese
best, sneezes

snuff.

II
Masks

God of the path-
way,
God of the
tree,
God of all part-
ing, we
greet you.

Your tree
has been split
by a white axe
of lightning;
the wise
are di-
vided, the
eyes
of our elders
are dead.

And we walk,
hope mock-
ing the path-
way, through the
dead leaves
of elders,
their dark eyes
of strangers di-
vided by pain
as by distance;
their wise
bones composed
into hallows
of silence;
lightnings flicker
through slits

where the sockets
once were;
rats'
teeth, spit-
ting fibre
have hollowed
the tree.

So the god,
mask of dreamers,
hears lightnings
stammer, hearts
rustle their secrets,
blood shiver like leaves
on his branches. Will
the tree, god
of path-
ways, still
guide us? Will
your wood lips speak
so we see?

III
Korabra

So for my hacked
face, hollowed eyes,
undrumming heart,

make me a black
mask that dreams
silence,

reflects no light,
smiles no pretence,
hears not my brother's

language.
Let me without
my mother's

blood, my father's
holy *kra*, traverse
paths where yet

the new dead
cannot know that
time was evil,

but where dew's
ears prepare
for my coming.

Back
through Elmina,
white granite stone

stalking the sun-
light, the dun-
geon unbars. I hear

the whips of the slavers,
see the tears
of my daughters;

over glass
of their shattered
cries, feet

bleeding, I walk
through the talk
of the market,

flies clotting
round en-
trails and trinkets.

Low voices murmur
like smoke; the *kenkey*
pots, drinking

gourds broken;
Asafoakye dance,
clay smeared

over fear, round
their arm-
pits; the white

cock's neck sac-
rifice fouled,
life twisted in

anger. Now the
village is gone
the castle col-

lapses in cloud.
Here now are the
thickets; leo-

pards cough
dust, snakes haul
rusty coils

from the road;
broad Akuapim
calls.

Here Nyame's
tree bent,
falling before the

Nazarene's cross.
Bells silenced the
gong-gong;

my spattered
cloth flapped
in its sound.

My scattered
clan, young-
est kinsmen,

fever's dirge
in their wounds,
rested here;

then limped on
down to their dungeon.
Cocoa grows now;

Koforidua quiet;
goats doze in the road-
way: des-

troying the years
with their chew-
ing impersonal stares.

V

Crossing the River

I
Bosompra

So crossing the river
and walking the path
we came at last to Kumasi.

You there on the other
bank, walking away
down the slope,

can you hear
can you hear me?
Cool river water

can you soothe
the wind's salt
scorching my eye,

blue finger of water,
heat's solace?
Can you hide me now

from the path's hope-
less dazzles, halts,
meetings, leaves' sudden

betrayal of silence, the sun's
long slant sloping
to danger?

I who have pointed my face
to the ships, the winds' anger,
today have returned, eat-

ing time like a mud-
fish; who was lost,
tossed among strangers,

waves' whitest con-
sonants, have returned
where the stones

give lips to the water:
asuo meresen
asuo meresen

asuo meresen...

II
Kumasi

city of gold,
paved with silver,
ivory altars,
tables of horn,

the morn-
ing sun of
seven hills
greets you best,

knows you blessed.
To the west
Denkyira dreams,
south the Akyems

seek their rest.
Asante Kotoko
Asante Kotoko
The drum grows

in the moon-
light, the porcupine
knows what is best;
Denkyira rests.

Kumasi

city of gold,
paved with silver,
ivory altars,
tables of horn,

the thorn
bush of love
bursts on the hill,
bleeds in the west,

knows you blessed.
To the best
of my dreams
I will sing

for your rest
Asante Kotoko
Asante Kotoko
The porcupine knows

it is too soon
for the hard
night to rest,
labours to nest.

Asante Kotoko
Asante Kotoko
Gold
will not rust,

silver grow dimmer,
diminish, show thinner;
but the ivory altars,
tables of horn,

will crack
with the day,
white finish glow
black,

bone's
body decay,
the blue gather thunder,
winds' lightnings bending and

snap-
ping the trees, blessed
crossroads of prayer,
the birds black.

Kumasi

city of gold,
paved with silver,
ivory altars,
tables of horn,

pray that the morn-
ing brings love;
the tilled
fields, blessed

shoots wrest-
led with rain; the west
dreams
of eager tipped wings.

Asante Kotoko
Asante Kotoko
Asante Kotoko
Buds close

in the moon-
light, the moon guards
the west;
Denkyira rests.

III

Tutu

1

And slowly slowly
ever so slowly

see how he slowly
comes to his feet

slowly slowly
ever so slowly

take care not to stumble
you of the palanquin;

see the bright symbols he's clothed himself in:
gold, that the sun may continue to shine

bringing wealth and warmth to the nation;
mirrors of brass to confound the blind

darkness; calico cloth to keep us from sin.
For Gyata the lion,

cracker of iron,
Atakora Firimpong,

who fought and seized kings,
black rock where the battle axe sings

Onoborobo with honour
Onoborobo with honour

Osai Tutu
is coming

'Birempon Tutu
is coming.

Whispers of dark
sasabonsam of darkness

will forever fear
his black rings of iron,

the rings
spiked with thorn.

2
So slowly slowly
ever so slowly

prepare for his coming;

bota beads, *bodom* beads
proclaim

his prosperity; red,
I am wealthy, my wealth

safe from termites;
and the feather, red

rooster, reminds us he
watches; the first one

who rises and the first one
who sings.

Spread the cloth in the path-
way.

Osee yei
Osee yei

Osee yei.

IV
The Golden Stool

1

Chiefs and people of the Asantehene
let all be well

All is well

Chiefs and people of the Asantehene
let all be well

We are listening

When the worm's knife cuts
the throat of a tree, what will happen?

It will die

When a cancer has eaten the guts
of a man, what will surely happen?

He will die

My people, that is the condition of our country today:
it is sick at heart, to its bitter clay.

We cannot heal it or hold it together from curses,
because we do not believe in it.
Like fighting cocks hungry for corn,

the highest crowded perches,
we are destroying our great nation.
Mampong says his shrines sit
heavier upon the snake,

time's coiled misfortune, than those at Berekum;
the Akyems will not care their own *sum-
an*; it is the same at Juaben;
their drums beat late on in the night, tall

reeds of coward's darkness:
hena beka, hena beka, hena beka hyen!
'Behind our wall, who dares to touch,
who dares to touch, who dares to touch us now!'

My people cannot collect tribute.

2

So down in thunder from his heaven
Anokye brought the Golden Stool.

Not since the mighty rule
of Nana Nyankopong began

had such excitements happened
in our town. Chiefs' sandalled

feet that never once had known
the ground, jumped from their palanquins

and ran; stools overturned,
noon's rule began; women,

moon's servitors, cool water's thoughts,
songs of before the forest,

dried, vanished underground.
Blood ruled and my cut tribe,

wailing like flutes,
whipped for their weakness,

brought to this red town.

For the tribe's
sake, the priests cried:

die: for the Stool's
honour, shrine's wealth,

lean slaver's health
of money. Do not seek

to find in the smoke's
mask of battle, your own

face, coward's eyes,
truth of fear.

For the tribe's
sake, the priests cried:

die. Let the tongues,
lips' labials, rot;

withering words in the hot
wind. If you must speak,

wear a black mask
of silence; ask-

ing no elder to lead you
again through the leaves,

through the path-
ways of prayer,

to Onyame's now
leafless air.

3

For I am the life of my people.
Like the cock
I produce shocks
of life

like the hen
I bear eggs when
the cycle is ripe: white

salt, tasteless soul
body, red yolk
where the meaty heart
beats.

And when the cycle is ripe
I, giver of life to my people,
crack open the skull, skill

of shell, care-
fully carved craft
of bones, and I kill.

VI
Arrival

I
Sunsum

So for my hacked
heart, veins' mem-
ories, I wear this

past I borrowed; his-
tory bleeds
behind my hollowed eyes;

on my wet back
tomorrow's sunlight dries;
welcome your brother now

my trapped curled tongue
still cries. And I return,
walking these burnt-

out streets, brain limp-
ing pain, masked
in this wood, straw

and thorns, seek-
ing the dirt of the com-
pound where my mother

buried the thin breed-
ing worm that grew
from my heart

to her sorrow. Some-
where under gravel
that black chord of birth

still clings to the earth's
warmth of glints, jewels' pressures, spin-
ning songs of the spider:

Kwaku Ananse who gleams
in the darkness
and captures our underground fears.

But my spade's hope,
shattering stone,
receives dumbness back

for its echo.
Beginnings end here
in this ghetto.

Firm fingers of shadow un-
mask me; my navel
string screams.

Can you hear
can you hear me,
blood's tissue,

curving issue
of cheek, bone
wrapped with breath, eyes

I remember so well?
Why did our gold, the sun's
sunsum, safe against termites, crack

under the white gun
of plunder, bright bridge-
head of money, quick bullet's bribe?

Why did the god's
stool you gave us,
Anokye,

not save us from pride,
foreign tribes' bibles,
the Christian god's hunger

eating the good of our tree;
flesh of my brothers' flesh
torn to feed ships,

profit's sea?
Too proud?
Too loud

in our white teeth
of praises?
Too rich?

Too external?
Too ready
with old ceremonial?

The years remain
silent: the dust learns nothing
with listening;

feet return to the stone,
pain of pathway: home-
less departer who stumbles on dark.

No longer here the wood crack-
ing, blue cooking smoke snap-
ping my anger of roads, sweat-

ing thickets. My sisters sip silence.
Brothers no longer notice.
My stool, tilted sideways, for-

gets slowly the slow press-
ing shape of my presence:
the termites' dark teeth, three

hundred years working,
have patiently ruined my art.

II

Tano

1

*Dam
dam
damirifa
damirifa due
damirifa due
damirifa due
due
due
due*

*Dam
dam
damirifa
damirifa due
damirifa due
damirifa due
due
due
due*

Whom does death overlook?
Whom
whom does death overlook?

I am an orphan
and when I recall the death
of my father

water from eyes
from my eyes
falls upon me

Dam
dam
damirifa
damirifa due
damirifa due
damirifa due
due
due
due

Dam
dam
damirifa
damirifa due
damirifa due
damirifa due
due
due
due

I am an orphan
and when I recall the death
of my mother

water from eyes
from my eyes
falls upon me.

We walk
we walk
we walk Nana Tano

and it will soon be night.

2

So Nana Tano
if I am going away now

you must help me.
Death,

dumb speaking god,
mutters for me;

deaf-
ness listens;

green hearing eyes see.
Exiled from here

to seas
of bitter edges,

whips of white worlds,
stains of new

rivers,
I have returned

to you.
Not Chad,

the Niger's blood,
or Benin's

burning bronze
can save me now.

You I depend upon:
Onyame's eldest son.

How have I failed
who only needed friends'

quick eyes to share
the terror?

How have I failed
who only tried to dare

the ships; slow journey's whips;
who speaks to me of error?

We walk
we walk

we walk, Nana Tano,
and it will soon be night.

3

And it will soon be night,
Nana Tano,

when the dry seed cracks
and a new star splits

into darkness. When the
drum sticks

bend and the drum-
mer climbs out of the dark-

ness. Buttocks balance
the earth; spine

fuses the drum-
beats to move-

ment; lights twinkle to life
in their root tips; the

tree rises
again and you rise

with its trunk and its move-
ment of branches; leaves

hear again what the distance is
saying; and my mem-

ory bends, curves, nods
head and crouches;

feeding the dust at the soles
of its feet as it dances.

III
The Awakening

Asase Yaa, Earth,
if I am going away now,

you must help me.
Divine Drummer,

'*Kyerema*,
if time sends me

walking that dark
path again, you

must help me.
If I sleep,

you must knock me
awake. . . .

And as the cock
now cries in the early dawn

so slowly slowly
ever so slowly

I will rise
and stand on my feet

slowly slowly
ever so slowly

I will rise
and stand on my feet.

Like *akoko* the cock
like *akoko* the cock

who cries
in the early dawn

akoko bon'opa
akoko tua bon

I am learning
let me succeed

I am learning
let me succeed...

Glossary

Aburi a town in Akuapim (q.v.) overlooking the Ga plains.
Ada (pronounced Adah), a town at the mouth of the Volta river, Ghana.
Adae an Akan ceremonial occasion.
adom (literally) favouring.
adowa a dance.
Agades a town in the western Sudan.
Akan the Twi-speaking people of Ghana: Ashanti, Akuapim, Fante, Akyem.
akoko cock
akoko bon anopa the cock crows in the early dawn (*anopa*).
akoko tua bon the cock rises and crows.
Akropong capital town of the Akuapim state.
Akuapim (or Akwapim), district and state between Ashanti and the coast, in eastern Ghana.
Akuse a town in the Ga state.
Akyem (or Akim), state and province in Ghana; formerly part of the Ashanti Federation.
Akyere Fante female name, suggesting revelation and also vindication.
Ananse the spider-hero of the Akans; earthly trickster, but once with powers of the creator-gods.
Anokye the *okomfo* or priest, traditionally held to have assisted at the divine creation of the Golden Stool of the Ashantis.
asafoakye warrior group (Ga); Akan *asafo*.
Asantehene king (*hene*) of the Ashanti (Asante) nation.
Asante Kotoko praise-name for the Ashanti nation; meaning invincible; see *kotoko*.
Asase Yaa the Akan Earth Goddess.
asuo meresen river, I am passing (crossing).
Atakora praise-name for the Asantehene. The first Atakora led the Ashanti against the Gyaman of the Ivory Coast.
atumpan talking drums.
Axum a town near the Red Sea, said to be the first nucleus of the Ethiopian kingdom.
Berekum division of the Ashanti Federation.
'Birempon praise-name, meaning mighty.
bodom beads multi-coloured pottery beads of great value.

Bosompra (or Pra), a river marking the boundary between the Fante and the Ashanti. According to tradition, Osai Tutu (q.v.) was killed crossing this river. Since then, under oath, the Asantehene is not supposed to cross this river.
bota beads   yellow coral beads worth their weight in gold.
Chaka   famous Zulu king and warrior.
damirifa due   condolences; the Akan sound of mourning. *Due* is pronounced *duē*.
Denkyira   rivals, in the seventeenth century, to the Ashanti.
duru   heavy, invincible.
eto   mashed plantain.
Ga   (pronounced Gah), coastal people between the Akuapim and the sea.
Golden Stool   symbol of the Ashanti nation.
Golokwati   a town in Ghana.
Gyata   lion; mighty, strong; praise-name for the Asantehene.
harmattan   seasonal wind from the Sahara desert.
Juaben   division of the old Ashanti Federation.
Kaneshie   a Ga village on the coast near Accra.
kenkey   a food.
Keta   a town on the extreme eastern coast of Ghana.
Kodia (or Kodua), appellation of power. Kodia was a famous Ashanti warrior-chief.
Koforidua   a town in Ghana, literally, *K'Ofori dua;* the place of Ofori's (holy) tree.
kon kon kon kon/kun kun kun kun   imitative of the sound of the drum. The passage in italics on p. 11 is from an Akan drum salutation.
Korabra   literally, 'go and come back'. The *korabra* is a signal drum often played at funerals.
kotoko   porcupine; see Asante Kotoko.
Kpandu   a town in Ghana.
kra   god-given spirit or soul.
Krachi   a town in Ghana.
Kumasi   capital of Ashanti.
Labadi   a Ga village.
Mampong   a state in the Ashanti Federation.
mmenson   an orchestra of seven elephant tusk horns used on state occasions to relate history.

Munia Muslim female name.
Naderina unattainable Paradise.
Nana title of respect.
Nana Firimpong name of an ancestor.
Nana Nyankopong the Creator.
nhima hima hima very very early.
nkyekyere Guinea grass.
Nsuta a town in Ghana.
Odomankoma with Onyame and Nana Nyankopong, a name of the Sky-God-Creator.
Odomankoma 'kyerema the Creator's drummer.
oko babi a he is ever-present.
onoborobo a drum call meaning assemble.
Onyame (or Nyame), the first name of the Supreme Being, the Creator.
Osai Tutu the royal founder of the Ashanti nation.
Osee yei shout of praise.
Ougadougou (or Wagadugu), one of the five Niger (Mossi) states.
Peki a town in Ghana.
Pong a town in Ghana.
Ra ancient Egyptian Sun God.
sasabonsam evil spirits.
Sokoto a town in what is now northern Nigeria.
suman fetish or charm.
sunsum spiritual blood.
Takoradi a seaport town in Ghana.
Tano a river sacred to the Akan.
Techiman (or Tekyiman) a town in northwestern Ashanti, near the source of the River Tano.
Teshie a Ga village.
Tutu see Osai Tutu.
tweneboa tree used for making drums; a kind of cedar.
Tweneboa Akore/Tweneboa Kodia praise-names used by the drums.
tweneduru as for *tweneboa*.
Volta Ghana's major river.
Walata a town in the western Sudan, once part of the ancient empire of Ghana.

wa ma ne-ho mene so oo   he is arising in all his majesty.
wawa, dahoma, esa, odum   names of trees.
Yeji   a ferry point on the river Volta between the northern savannah and the Ashanti forest.

*Printed in
Great Britain
by
The Bowering Press
Plymouth*

DATE DUE